ACKNOWLEDGEMENT

My thanks to Rachel McCue, Richel Dillard, and Alyna Karczmar for helping with some editing. It's always hard to produce anything in a vacuum and finding out in advance what does and does not work is always helpful. Thank you all for your time and effort. It is greatly appreciated!

Really Bad Poems From a Loud Librarian

Karissa Davison

Presentation by *BookLeaf Publishing*

Web: www.bookleafpub.com

E-mail: info@bookleafpub.com

ISBN: 9789357742504

First edition 2023

PREFACE

Alternative titles for this volume include:

T-Rex Just Wants a Hug

It's Not Poetry Unless It Comes From the Poetry Region of France; Then It's Just Lyric Prose

Alice Revisited

All was not tea
That the doormouse was steeped in
As he sat in his teapot
And waited for her

The smoke from the hookah
Curled 'round his nose
Making the world
Softer to know

He watched the Mad Hatter
Natter and Natter,
Pouring tea on the crumpets
Until they were soggy and wet

He knew she was coming
And would know when she came
But stayed in his pot
Because his friends were lame

It was freedom he sought
From the cave and the darkness
Into light and air and the music of silence
A freedom of movement he had missed for years

But the lid fit his head
And the smoke made him sleepy
And watery pastries were all
That he knew

Norse Shanty

There once was a man that I did know
Who came from a land of ice and snow
There was not a thing he did not know
His ravens told him after

He gave them his eye so he could see
And they would tell him of all the glorious
things
Out through the trees and across the sea
And the snow'd come storming after

Oh ho, the Gods they grow
Out from the land of wind and snow
Oh ho, the darkness flows
Over the deep volcanoes

Then there was a lass who caught the eye
Of the man who was friends with the crows that
cry
And for her heart he did so vie
His wife forever after

She was a powerful witch woman
With a boar as a pet, and battles won
And a herd of cats to pull her on

For war and graceful laughter

Oh ho, the Gods they grow
Out from the land of wind and snow
Oh ho, the darkness flows
Over the deep volcanoes

Prayer for Others

For my people
My loves
My family
I want them safe
And fed
And loved
I want them at my table
Bathed in Light and Joy

For those who are not my people
Though their choices are not mine
I want them safe
And Fed
And Loved
At their own tables
Surrounded by their own people
Bathed in Light and Joy

For those friends shared by both of us
May they travel in love
and find Joy and Comfort in the company they
keep
Whether at my table
Or another

Platonic

There is a story
About a cave
Where all the people live
Watching shadows dance
On walls made of darkness
And rock
Calling it
Life
or
Reality

But some wander from the cave
Into the brightness of day
With warm breezes
Flowers and clouds
Animals scuttling under brush
The scent of jasmine and sunshine
And those who see the light
Return to the darkness
To tell the others of the
World Outside

But the people in the cave

Do

Not
Care

They don't believe anything could be better
Than the things they see on the wall
Flickering and fleeting
Dancing but untouchable
Watching the story
They are being told is true

And the people
Who saw the Light
Tried to pull the others out

Away from their lotus dreams
And the safety of the cave
The comfort of the darkness
The solidity of Stone all around them
The familiarity of the shadows that hold them

It's for your own good.

I am happy here.

It's not real.

Who says?

I do. I've seen more.

I have seen better.

Why does there have to be more?
I am happy here.
This is where I made my life.
You are trying to take
The life I have made
And turn it to dust
And I will fight you
Beyond my death
To save myself
From your lies.
This is where I want to stay
And this is where
I will bury the bodies
Of any who try
To take what is mine.

And the people
Who had seen the light
Looked around the cave
Unable to stay
Not wanting to die
Here
Surrounded by darkness
With light and freedom
So close
They could smell the grasses waving
Dancing in gusts

Of little breezes

And they let their friends
Live
In the darkness of their own making
Hoping
That someday the light would call
To those left behind

On Writing Here

There seems to be a theme
Of Darkness
Into Light
Where darkness is bad
And cold
And ignorant
Where Light is good
And warm
And kind
And loving
And All Things Good

But is that really how it is?

I love the darkness physically
The hinderance of sight
The warmth of blankets and animals around me
The softness of bed and pillows and couch
The safety of
Not Having To Deal With The World
The limited bullshit of being on my own

Light hurts
It makes me leave my comfort
And go out into the world

Deal with people
Places
Things
Make decisions
Adult
THINK

Light is a struggle
Uphill
Both ways
In the snow
Up to your knees
With only one shoe
Blinding you as it bounces off
A crisp winter earth
Making you sneeze
In Brightness

There is warmth in sunlight
True
And a shadow-dappled meadow
Is full of Life
And promise
And Hope
And a million tiny lives all working to survive

But sometimes I want less
Less light
Less stress

Less thought
Just being

And for that, darkness helps

We Call It Cannabis Because We're Fancy

I think too much

About EVERYTHING

My therapist agrees

Yes, I am self-aware
I accept responsibility
For all of my bad decisions
And probably some that are
Out of my control
I think about how my actions
Effect
Those around me
Though sometimes I am too late
And the damage is already done
Which means now
I also get to think about how much I've failed
And how much more I have to try to be better
And Grow
And try to become
Someone Else
Who is better
Kinder

Wiser
Than this pile of messiness
I am constantly on the verge of becoming
Because a messy pile
Is still better
Than the load of uselessness
I've been my whole life

And no,
I do not accept
Constructive criticism
At least as far as
My failures
Are concerned

And yes,
I am that failure
Ruined
Broken
Destructive
Hateful
Antagonistic
Rightfully despised
Just plain awful

I once read a fable
About a woman
Who had a bad story inside of her
That made her act

Against her own best interest
Making the bad tale,
Which had originally had no basis in reality,
Into a self-fulfilling prophecy

Perhaps I am also this woman,
Told as a child I was
Too much
Too thoughtless
Too fat
Too useless
In word and deed and thought and breath
Unhelpful
Unkind
Unthinking

Constantly spinning
Drowning in
Awareness
Of my Self
And my place in the world
Reliving all failures
Never retaining anything
That might make my own continued existence
Anything less
Than a burden
On everyone around me

AND THEN

Something to make the voices quieter
Something to smooth the edges
Something to help me let go
And forgive myself for mistakes,
Even if it's only for a little while
Something to make me laugh
Or at least smile
(if a bit blankly and vapidly)

Because after more than forty years
Of constant self-inflicted suffering
Being able to take a little break
A few hours every day
Means I will probably
Keep going
For awhile longer

Under My Skin

Today I will have
Ink
Placed in my skin
Colors swirling
And blending
Into something beautiful

Without the ink
or the pain
I would be left with
Nothing
To do
But
Slice the skin from my arms
And legs
A strip at a time
And the only beauty left of me
Would be a bloodstain
On the floor

Curly Girl Out of Light

My hair grows
Long and heavy
Curls pulling straight
Losing its self
As it twines lower and lower
Always seeking its lowest level
Pulling me down with it

My eyes used to see
So far in the light
Blue and green and grey
Taking on details
Cataloging the beauty and ugliness alike
Drawing me upward
To cloud and treetop
Where the wind would whistle past my ears
Singing in my air
But blinding me to everything around me
If only for a moment

I once felt joy
In sunlight
But now I am left tired and burned
Skin and soul
Ears and eyes

Hair bleached of happiness
Curls long gone
Pulled straight and brittle
Without my notice

My Family Before

My mother thinks she's dying
She tells my father
Mum's the word
But we know

We feel it

We worry
And our hearts break
Because there is nothing to be done

I made friends with my own Death,
But not with the those of others

You are not me
You cannot leave
The world needs you here

I do as I please
Who gave you permission to go on without me?

I long to wear them on my skin,
The sisters from other misters I have claimed as
my own
The cousins who hold me tight in their hearts

The aunts and uncles who think me dear
All becoming armor
Against my own darkness

My family is forged of ink and
Love and choice
And I will find strength and solace in them

I think of my mother
and wonder
if she's given enough
Suffered enough
Lived in this world enough
Loved us all hard enough
That she will stay with us
In our blood
Even after she's gone

There are Bad Aunts, and then there are Bad Aunts

I am an auntie
It is one of my favorite roles to fill
I adopt children from friends
To be my nieces and nephews
Because claiming them as my own
Lets me surround them with
The love of my heart
And offer them the safety
They might sometimes need

I think about my aunt
Who disowned one child,
Who would pick and choose who was worthy of
being loved
And who was not
Who would disown me, too,
If only it meant
She wouldn't then lose the power she holds over
me,
The power I give her
Without my own permission.
Her disinterest and distaste for me is colossal
In my formative years

I never understood why my sister was held so
close to her heart
Held in a halo of love and light
While I was left alone
What did I do
As a child
To earn her scorn?
Why do I let her keep the strength she took from
me?
She still searches for me
At family gatherings
Not to see how I making it through this life,
But to make sure her beloveds are still doing
better

I do not want other children
To feel the scorn of an elder
Making them feel
That they are too hard to love
When all they are doing
Is trying to be
The most
Themselves
That they can be
This life is hard enough
Without having someone whispering in your ear
That nothing you do is right
And you are not good enough
To be loved

The Opposite of Love is Indifference

The problem with Libras,
And probably with most air signs,
Is that we are all-or-nothing people
There is very little middle ground
Either we love you with our whole hearts
Or we want to see you planted in the ground
And sometimes it's hard to tell
Which way we want you

If we love you,
We will probably love you forever
To the edge of eternity and back again
Twice times infinity
With all of our hearts, minds, and souls
Inside of every cliché
Men have created
To define the passions of their tiny hearts
In the vast Galaxy
Of multi-dimensional bubbles of all the realities

If we hate you,
It will probably be
With the same passion
That will make the fires of Hell

Look like picnic weather
On a clear day in spring
On a blanket shared by frolicking baby animals
With sunscreen really nearby

But it's never the hatred that should concern you
Because with the right shift of weather
Or the wrong level of betrayal,
Our feelings may change
From passion, either love or hate,
To nothing

With nothing,
I am free of you
Unburdened by concern for you
Uncaring of anything you might experience
Unwilling to expend the energy it takes
To care whether you live or not

It is a relief and a release
From which you will never return
Because why would I pick up a chain
When I can exist
Without you pulling me down?
Why bother loving or hating you forever
When I can live freely and lightly
Without in my world?

To Someone, You Are Toxic, Too

When it is my turn to be cast out
Ignored
Blocked
Avoided,
I understand,
Completely and Intuitively
How deeply I have wounded you

Sometimes that is the only way I will learn
That the weight I gave you to carry
Crushed your spirit
And the only way around
That crushing neutrality
Is for me to bang against
The boundary you built between us
You want to be free of the weight of my crimes
That I committed
Either with or without my knowledge or
understanding

I wish only for you
The freedom of indifference to me
That I might not hurt you again
Though the knowledge of my own betrayal

Will sit in my heart
Like a stone weight
Threatening to drown me
As I deserve

Just because I did not mean it
Does not mean you have to
Forgive or Forget
And I have to learn to be ok with that
Though I will miss you
With all my might

Gen Z and the Destruction of the Universe As We Know It

In all honesty,
Watching the next generation
Tear down so many societal norms
Is fascinating.

So many ideas
We were taught were sacred
Have been being pulled out
Held up to the light
And discarded like the trash they have always
been

The youngsters are going to Marie Condo the
world
And I
Am
Here
For It!

Two of the worst moments
In high school
Was being asked
In the lunch line
If I was a boy or a girl.

The shame of being a chunky girl,
One whose curves curved wrong,
Turned my cheeks scarlet
And my eyes to the floor
Not just in shame,
But in rage
That someone could ask a question
So stupid
And hurtful
And not really care about the answer.

I am lucky
That my sense of self
Has always matched
My gender,
But my heart breaks for those people
Who were born in the wrong bodies
With the wrong attachments
Who had to go out into the world
And pretend nothing was wrong
While never feeling comfortable
In their own skin

The children are teaching us
To Be Who We Are
Regardless of the trappings of our meat suits
They understand that this Death World is HARD
And if something makes it worse, it's ok to say
no

And that is energy we need more of
As our reality rushes to its end.

Kindness is Power

I read something that pointed out
That there is a difference between
Being Nice
and
Being Kind

Being Nice is performative
Full of thoughts and prayers
Tearful candle vigils
Stuffed animals left
At the site of destruction
Smiling while weeping
Sitting by and waiting for help to arrive
Covered in an emergency blanket
That proves you've really
Been
Through
Something
Traumatic

Being Kind is active
Finding solutions
Perhaps with a touch of tough love
Followed by the choice
To Do Something Useful

Solve the problem
Being proactive and creative to save others
From having to experience something painful

This is why people
Are called to be Kind
Kindness is dangerous
A fierce kind of love
One that may involve yelling in frustration
But will ultimately
Bring to light
A solution
An opportunity to heal

They say
You cannot be peaceful
Unless you are dangerous
If you do not have the power
Of great destruction
You are not peaceful,
You are harmless
You can only be Nice

Be Powerful
Be Dangerous
Be Kind

Gifts and Curses Are Two Sides of the Same Coin

My actual gift is not the gift of gab.
Though I speak
And comfort
And teach
With gentleness and concern and caring.
My gift is the gift of harsh truths.
I hear the words in my head and know if I say
them
out loud
they will devastate you.

Without a thought
I can tell you the unvarnished truth.
I know exactly what words in what order will
best destroy you.
Because I can see your fears and your pain and
your insecurities.
I can do it without a thought.
The truths just slip out,
around the corners of my teeth,
from behind a smile,
laughter in my eyes,
and I stab you in your secret heart,
the one you hope no one knows about,

that one fear that you hope isn't true.
But I can see it and I can hear it
and
if I'm not careful,
so will you.

It's a blow to the gut.
I've done it to myself,
by myself,
a million times before.
I've said the thing that hurts the worst,
just to watch myself bleed.
Maybe if I say it, it won't be true.
Maybe if I say it,
it will be a lie that I can hear,
a discord in the harmony
But it never is.
I hear the truth of the words,
the sharpness of the syllables,
and I know that I can cut you from navel to
neck,
spilling your secret fears for everyone to see,
a wash of your blood to coat the world.
And I'll feel bad about it.

Probably.

We'll hear the truth and know it for what it is.
Unkindness

Cruelty
Monsterousness
Fun
My dark heart revels in your spilling blood,
the light of your soul getting a little darker as
you acknowledge my words.
It was not a joke,
though we both play it off as one,
chuckling
like you're not bleeding to death in the middle of
the room,
like I'm not watching you die on the inside
Like I didn't just say the one thing you hoped no
one would ever think,
let alone say.

My tongue is sharp and it will cut us both to
ribbons
Because even as I hurt you
I hurt myself
I feel your pain as if it is my own
And I know exactly how I hurt you and how
deeply it cut
And I am sorry
Am sorry
Am sorry
But there is nothing I can ever do to fix what I
have done
So I just keep my mouth shut

My eyes shut
My face blank
Because if I look at you, you will see the words
there
The words I refuse to say out loud
The words that will kill you between heartbeats
Because I don't want to be that girl
Even though she lives just beneath my skin
Waiting for me to give in to distraction
So she can say the things no one needs to hear
And bathe in the blood of your heart
While you and I try to laugh it back in

Burdens

I collect so many thing
Mugs and bowls
Glass and ceramic
Shot glasses and magnets
Ideas and images

I put them in my pockets
Because fat lady pants
Actually give us the chance
To make our hips stick out further
With pockets that can hold
Phones
Rocks
Other people's expectations
The stress of not fitting
Physically
Into the world we live in

So many people look at heavy people,
Especially women,
As if we are some kind of science experiment
Why are we fat?
Don't we care about our health?
Why don't we eat better?
Or exercise more?

Or care about our appearance?
Or try, even a little bit, to lose
All
That
Weight?

But the truth is
There are worse things than being fat.
I could be unkind
I could be selfish
I could be hateful
I could be stupid
And people who encourage me,
And others like me,
To fight to reshape the form
We have been using
Throughout this lifetime
Don't understand
That just because I am bigger than you like
Does not mean
That I am lacking

Less may sometimes be more
But sometimes more
Is just enough to survive

Red-Headed Stranger: A Haiku

Botticelli's girl
The one with long Titian hair
Rests within the world

End Game

I came to have fun
For however long it is
I wish time would fly

9 789357 742504